IMAGINE MY LIFE

Poetry by

JAMES SANTORA

Dedication

Imagine My Life is dedicated to Donna, my wife and best friend, who hates poems that do not rhyme. I also want to thank my sister-in-law Angela for her continued support and Robin E. Devonish Scott for helping me remove one item from my bucket list. Last, I would like to add one more dedication, of course, to every person who has ever lived.

Dedication

Imagine My Life is dedicated to Donna, my wife and best friend, who hates poems that do not rhyme. I also want to thank my sister-in-law Angela for her continued support and Robin E. Devonish Scott for helping me remove one item from my bucket list. Last, I would like to add one more dedication, of course, to every person who has ever lived.

Imagine My Life

PUBLIC RELATIONS

I once wrote a book
of five hundred blank pages
and dedicated it to every person
who has ever lived;
you can find it
in every bookstore
in every library
between every bookend
almost everyone has a copy
but no one has ever read
past the dedication
and five hundred essays
have been written on it
the critics praise the work
while the people ask for the sequel
and they want to give me an award
but I am too busy with the revision
editing where I can.

BIRTH

Once,
A thousand years ago
I told you
the beach was wet
with juices
You laughed at my simplicity.

Now,
The sea sends a request
and slowly
I remove my clothes
and swim
against the tide
toward the island
where I was born
while knowing
my arms
haven't the power
to reach it.

All I can think of
as I melt
into the ocean
is your laughter
ages ago
when your heart
touched my mind
leaving its impression
petrified
until now.

PROTECTIVE BALANCE

SPONTANEOUS
The sand has not known
the fire
has not known
the pressure
but I can feel the breath closing the jaws
drawing the saliva
from the mouth
of Earth.

The sand surrounds the ocean
takes its moisture
for its own thirst
never anxious to give it back.
The sand is guilty and sentenced
when we take it away
to make the infant
we call glass.

You cannot expect
ice cream to melt in December,
but come July
it must surrender
to the inevitable.

PLANNED

The sand surrounds the ocean
takes moisture
for its own thirst
never anxious to return it
keeping it for days
until the sun
sends judgment.
During the process
we steal the sand away
plunder and rape it
to breed the infant
we call glass.

Then, on a windy night
Sometime in December
a branch falls
through a window.
It is one a.m.
The hardware store has been
closed for six hours.

SPLIT ENDS

Have you ever wondered
where the hairs
that clog every drain go?
Maybe, they have a meeting
somewhere in a cesspool
contemplating whether
some bald men
deserve another chance.

STEW

I asked for conversation
You gave me asparagus

I asked for compassion
You gave me broccoli

I asked for understanding
You gave me carrots

I asked for intimacy
You gave me mashed potatoes

I asked for strength
You gave me spinach

I asked for commitment
You gave me string beans

Why is it that whenever
I want to talk
You give me vegetables
You passed the corn and said, "Eat!"

MOTHERHOOD

Read between the stretch marks
The thirty-two hour massaging
     of all the fears and expectations
     passed by limbs and loins
     of her to me as I to you
I waited for transition
     to rear its violent head
     parched by decaying breath
     and the never-ending itch of anxiety
Finally the pushing
     peeling scotch tape from a window
Surfing emotion
Extra sensory placenta dresses my thoughts
     for the tomorrow that is today
The episiotomy delivers
You appear with your life in my bosom
One day you will be afraid of the pain,
     the commitment and
I will lay you close to my bosom once again
Telling you how much I love you
     and you will understand the miracle.

PRIDE

I will not have
my balloon filled
by a company
of insincere operators.

The work is much too difficult
to entrust to unknowns.

The insurance
will not cover
fire and theft
since I will never get
close enough to the flame and
it is much too easy a target
to be removed.

I will use my own breath
and protect it
with all the safeguards
I feel necessary.
If it bursts
or is stolen,
it will be
my own fault.

BODY LANGUAGE

Yellow jaw dice

ankle oh sore us

you're under a wrist

joint seen nothing yet

pre-knuckles agreement

lit elbow peep

I'll buy it on con spine mint

tibia or not tibia

fun knee!

SURPRISE!

It was a red letter day
You, I
Diamonds are forever, so it's said
In the refrigerator
    no, you like to eat out on Thursdays
Under the pillow,
    no, you may fall asleep on the couch
Dixie cup surprise,
    no, you always rinse without
The hall closet,
    no, you'll place your coat on the knob
Your pink slip, I mean robe,
    you always put that on as soon as you
    get home
That's it!
    and as I lifted the robe off the bed,
There was a note
    written on a yellow sheet of paper
    probably a grocery list you forgot to
    give me
Dear John,

THE FIRST CHILD
...............STILLBIRTH

B rok en chairs
        the hunter has clawed at trees,
they got in the way

Crac ked glass
        the beachcomber grinds and curses,
the sand is not silver

S e p a r a t i o n   breeds in pieces.

Someone has drawn the consideration
while making the bed

The refrigerator is out of milk.
The house is out of toilet paper.

On the floor
        a stunt ed cigar bleeding
onto a hole in the carpet

The groceries are wet
        a child is crying in a cottoned room

The lock is doored up.

"How many children do you have? ... the judge asked

"None." was the reply.

The first is dead.

SPACE JOURNAL

PAGE ONE:

Isolation!

the sound of water

constantly dripping

whether beneath the sunset

or above the rise.

The perfect state!

this hermit permanently running

exploring iron mines

with unexpected companions.

The persistence!

this waste through indifference

is only waste when it is seen.

To the hermit, it's another journey.

The moon is getting larger every day

the air is pure

between us lies

wires, space and

the perception

from a sharper angle.

Let your sink run

damn the future

from here

I can see your oceans evaporating.

PAGE TWO: Space Journal

I've been too long for the moon

being alone and

having nothing else to do

but make love to her.

I have never made love

to a silver woman

or to someone round.

I eject myself

and float above her.

The Earth is turning

red and green

with each rotation

and I

am complacent

knowing it is

just you and I,

silver woman.

PAGE THREE: Space Journal

Circling

unconscious yet robotized

like the button I'm pushing.

I obey the scientific rules

man has contracted with machine.

I surrender myself

to my ship's desires

turning off the radio.

I can hear them calling

as my heat melts the circuit.

I have broken the contract

"Switching to manual control!"

TRUTH

My eye turns
a void
of painted ideas
and still-life cartoons
hiding in caves
torches lit
burning the dust
accumulated from
years of abandonment

A light vein spreads

My eye hangs
on a summit
a cloud of captured light
appears
followed

by colored sound
circling like a madman
until it is enclosed
within the cloud

The picture is unclear

My eye strains
for contrast;
the cloud dims
a fine mist passes
it rises

My eye glances
but it is gone

My eye turns
disappointed
back into place.

THE FALL

Unless the ice
was in the cradle
the rocking
would be faster
a greater tendency
to fall
destroying the soft skin
the skull having
no defense
no way of breaking
the fall.

The wood splatters
leaving its memories
upon the cliff
and all that's left
is the nakedness
of a child's body
and the simplicity
of earth.

If the ice was there
the mixture
of gold and silver
would produce concealed
air holes from which
the ice could drip
without suspect
and the cradle
eventually would slip.

The fall would be
a comfortable slide
and the child
would not had known
it had fallen.

SPLINTERS

The grain in wood
is straight up and down
Going against it
would cause splinters
Be careful to know
the grain's direction
Or make sure it's
so highly polished
that it doesn't
notice your
touch.

ASBESTOS

Fifties

the insulation of asbestos

strong leadership and solid government

like steel crackers in soup

corporate boom sonically

technology breeds recreation

get married, have children, retire

the home is safe

Sixties

an awakening mischievousness

the dandruff flakes of corrosion

beacon the irony of indifference

the shot, the war, the restiveness

music replaces blood

live together, have children, protest

the home shows signs of wear

Seventies

newspaper living

pollution, shortages, boycotts

secret cementized plots

breaking in, breaking out

green veins protrude

get married, have a child, divorce

the home installs an alarm system

Eighties

the asbestos must be removed

sensitivity is given a bedtime story

restless nights conjure answers

that go questioned

alien intravenous, skyscraper mentality

date, work, travel

the home doesn't have a nursery

Nineties

the asbestos was purged

by the electromagnetic undertaker

we stand naked at the mirror

will we rush to be clothed or

go home to rebuild.

SLICE OF LIFE

A woman
      dressed in black
      carrying one child
      another tugging at her skirt
      pushing a stroller

It's been years
      since anyone
      told her how beautiful she is
It's been decades
      since she believed it

Another night, another drink
another man … another moment
the reach is deeper

Howard Beach
Bensonhurst
Headlines miss her again

I am NOT sliced bread!!!

DRAMAS OF THE DRYING WASHBOARD

I am watching
dramas of the drying washboard
being annoyed that
someone is sweeping
high quality dust
with a cheap broom

The paneling of my mind
dresses tomorrow for my children
and the food
is being cooked evenly

My dreams are sleeping
under the covers
of the neatly made bed

Do not leave me
fresh fruit
It will only go bad.

FILL

Nothing is empty
that can be filled

I touch the burnt fibers
of an old dust rag
This reminds me of faith

I touch the rough edges
of plaster chips
This reminds me of patience

I see walls
hitting the ground as ashes
This reminds me of passion

I see the knife
slicing the air behind me
This reminds me of courage

I smell the dead flesh
still walking inside the flames
This reminds me of endurance

I taste the odor of decadence
around every corner
This reminds me of strength

And finally
a chance
to fill.

THE CALENDAR WOMAN

The morning's breath
unlocks a door
I enter being baptized
from the dew on tattered curtains.

A lady with orange-peel skin
motions that I come sit by rags
amid my daughter's lost teddy bear.
On her right, a negative of a photograph
On her left, a mirror reflecting
a stone bleeding milk
in a field of gray grass
a sky green-black
It is raining dead roses.

The calendar woman hands me a paper
written in Old Greek
a recipe for tomorrow's birthday cake

My daughter's anniversary.
On the same day, my dog
will cough hysterically
and die.

THE CORNER

No one bothers to look
inside the drawer
I hide in a corner
just getting enough
air to breathe
and the underwear
gives me nutrition
to stand the pressure
of the pajamas
falling on top of me
If I could only get out
perhaps I would
show them how to
match socks properly
the disarrangement puts
my nerves on edge, sometimes
so much so that I stretch out
the elastic on the shorts
If only someone …

THE TURNING OF CHEEK

A child born
water is injected
carefully and continually
into its cheek

A child growing
taking a drink
being scolded for it
water runs down its cheek

A child older
giving water
a passing stream
to family, friends
quickly without satisfaction

A child older yet
playing in the ocean
getting wet
touching water
to the cheeks of strangers

Maturity
the cheek becomes
inflated, fully moistened
until the burst and seepage
slowly through the years
through the allowances promised

The last drippings
are cherished
but cannot break the thirst

The cheek is dry
being occasionally wet at times
for gratitude
for memory.

INHIBITIONS

Were you blind
        as leaves to moonlight
        all the endless recollections
        have the power to create
        relevant activity; hidden lines
        fear no constrained frustrations.
Are you one
        to expect chilled sliding
        from a cradle in the dark
        leaving your vanity to
        empty tables, your gratitude
        to half-filled glasses.

Will you succumb
        to intentions
        formless upon mosaic tiles
        half your past lies in
        the sculpture of dead movements
        violent branches broken
        by unfelt arrows
        piercing through your virginity.

DUST

The dust
    slowly escaped the
    vacuum cleaner this morning.
    It hid by the living room nook
    where it was sure
    of not being noticed.
    There was a close call last week
    under the welcome mat.

The dust and I
    we keep moving
    hiding in small corners
    each weekend
    admiring our courage
    knowing it's futile
    but running anyway.

EXIT

I only believe in
     exit signs
They give me a
     sense of security
I always know
     which way is out.